KALEIDOSCOPE

Earthquakes

Joe Thoron

 **Marshall Cavendish**
Benchmark
New York

Marshall Cavendish Benchmark
99 White Plains Road
Tarrytown, New York 10591-9001
www.marshallcavendish.us

All Internet sites were available and accurate when sent to press.

Library of Congress Cataloging-in-Publication Data
Thoron, Joe.
Earthquakes / by Joe Thoron.
p. cm. — (Kaleidoscope)
Includes bibliographical references and index.
ISBN-13: 978-0-7614-2102-3
ISBN-10: 0-7614-2102-5
1. Earthquakes—Juvenile literature. I. Title. II. Series: Kaleidoscope (Tarrytown, N.Y.)
QE521.3.T548 2007   551.22—dc22   2006003087

Editor: Marilyn Mark
Editorial Director: Michelle Bisson
Art Director: Anahid Hamparian
Series Designer: Adam Mietlowski

Photo Research by Anne Burns Images
Cover Photo by Photo Researchers/D.Parker

The photographs in this book are used with permission and through the courtesy of: *Corbis*: p. 1, 19 Kimimasa Mayama/Reuters;
p. 4 Lloyd Cluff; p. 12 Crack Palinggi/Reuters; p. 28 Oliver Matthys/epa; p. 32 Roger Ressmeyer; p. 35 Shahpari Sohaie; p. 36
Stringer/Malaysia/Reuters; p. 40 James Robert Fuller; p. 43 Erico Sugita/Reuters. *Photo Researchers Inc.*: p. 7 Gary Hincks/Science Photo
Library; p. 8 Simon Fraser; p. 16 Martin Bond/Science Photo Library; p. 24 British Antarctic Survey/Science Photo Library. *U.S. Geological
Survey*: p. 11, 15 U.S. Dept. of Interior; p. 31 C.J. Langer. *Art Resource*: p. 20 Erich Lessing. *NOAA*: p. 27 NGDC. *Getty Images*: p. 39

Printed in Malaysia
6 5 4 3 2 1

Contents

Earthquake!

Earthquakes are among nature's deadliest disasters. They strike without warning. The ground shakes and rumbles for seconds or even minutes. Furniture topples. Houses slide off their foundations. Trees and power lines crash to the ground. Bridges collapse.

In the United States, up to 75 million people living in thirty-nine states are at risk of being in a serious earthquake. Are you one of them?

This elevated freeway in Oakland, California, collapsed in the 1989 Loma Prieta earthquake.

An earthquake is a sudden shaking of the ground caused by a movement under the Earth's surface. The buildup of extraordinary stresses in the rocks that make up the Earth's *crust* brings about this movement.

This image shows the underground location of an earthquake (the focus point is shown here as a red dot) and how shock waves spread out through the Earth's crust.

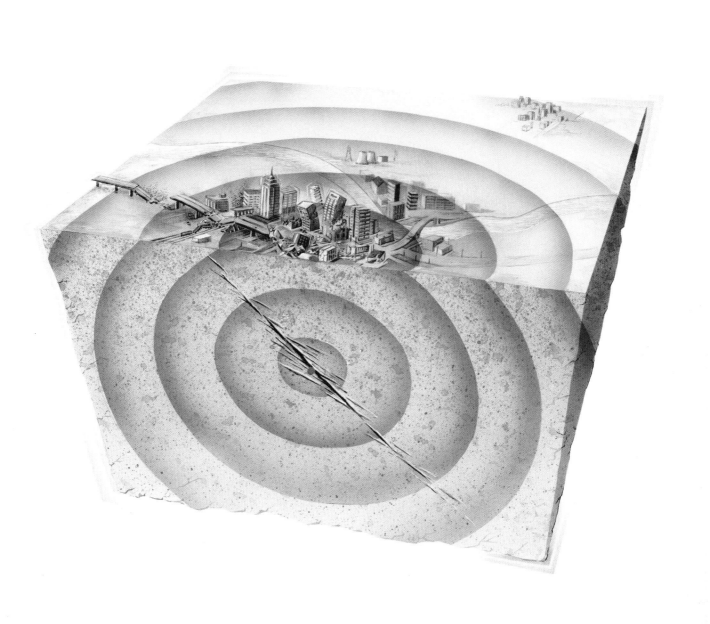

The Earth's crust is made up of about twelve to twenty large pieces, called *tectonic plates*. These plates move slowly around the globe (more slowly than your fingernails grow). Where they meet, they grind against each other, building up stress in all of the surrounding rocks. Eventually the stress is too much for the rocks to withstand and they suddenly shift along a *fault*. Sometimes the two plates slide past each other horizontally, and sometimes one plate goes up while the other plate goes down.

The North American and European tectonic plates meet near Þingvellir, Iceland. The two plates are slowly moving apart. The last major earthquake on this fault occurred in 1789.

Earthquakes begin at a *focus point,* or *hypocenter,* many miles down in the Earth's crust. The rupture then moves along the fault like a zipper, at speeds of hundreds or thousands of miles per hour. The longer the rupture, the stronger the earthquake.

The northwest side of the Hanning Bay fault in Prince William Sound in Alaska (right side of photo) moved upward as much as 16 feet (4.8 m) during the Great Alaskan earthquake of 1964.

Many of the world's strongest earthquakes occur in *subduction zones*. These are areas where a heavier *oceanic plate* is being pushed underneath a lighter *continental plate*. The deadly 1960 Chilean quake, which is the largest ever recorded, and the 2004 Indian Ocean quake, one of the deadliest, occurred in subduction zones.

◀ *Rubble from the March 31, 2005, earthquake in Indonesia.*

Earthquakes can also occur in the middle of large tectonic plates. The New Madrid earthquakes of 1811 and 1812 struck the area where Missouri, Tennessee, and Kentucky meet at the Mississippi River, far from the boundary of any tectonic plates. These quakes changed the course of the Mississippi River and shook the Earth so strongly that the *shock waves* made church bells ring as far away as Boston.

While earthquakes can sometimes relieve the stress on nearby rocks, they often do not ease all the stress in an area. *Aftershocks* are small earthquakes that occur after a larger earthquake. About one-third of all detected earthquakes are aftershocks. Most aftershocks take place in the first few days after a quake, and quickly become less frequent.

These trees near Reelfoot Lake in Tennessee were tilted by the New Madrid earthquakes.

▶

Earthquake Science

In an earthquake, the movement of the Earth's crust creates *seismic waves* in all directions, just as a pebble does when it is dropped into a pond. Some seismic waves travel deep into the Earth and can be detected worldwide. Others travel on the surface of the Earth, either shaking the ground from side to side or making the surface roll up and down like ocean waves.

Scientists who study earthquakes are called *seismologists*. They use machines called *seismographs* to detect shock waves moving through the Earth. By analyzing the shock waves they can figure out where an earthquake started and how strong it was.

◀ *Along this road, which cuts through the San Andreas fault in California, the layers of rock have been twisted and folded by earthquakes. This fault is the boundary between the Pacific and the North American plates.*

When people talk about the strength of an earthquake, they give it a number, such as 5.0, 6.1, or 7.7. This is the *magnitude* of the earthquake, and is a measurement of its total energy. Many scales have been used to detect an earthquake's magnitude. The *Richter scale*, developed in 1935, is the most widely known. Today, most scientists use the *moment-magnitude scale* to describe earthquakes because it is much more precise than other scales. This scale uses exact measurements made at the fault before and after the quake.

A quake measuring 5.0 is considered a moderate quake and can be felt by people but doesn't usually do much damage. More than one thousand of these quakes occur worldwide each year. The Great Chilean earthquake of 1960 measured 9.5, and is the largest earthquake ever reported.

This chart shows the frequency of different sizes of earthquakes. The data is from the National Earthquakes Information Center of the U.S. Geological Survey. ▶

Frequency of Earthquakes throughout the World

Descriptor	Magnitude	Annual Average
Very minor	2–2.9	1,300,000
Minor	3–3.9	130,000
Light	4–4.9	13,000
Moderate	5–5.9	1,319
Strong	6–6.9	134
Major	7–7.9	17
Great	8 or higher	1

In addition to measuring present-day quakes with seismographs, seismologists can estimate the strength of quakes that occurred in ancient times. One of the best ways to study ancient earthquakes is to dig trenches across a fault line and examine the layers of soil and rock to see where and how far they have been separated. Fragments of trees or plants found in the layers of soil can help determine when the quake happened. The history of a fault's earthquakes gives seismologists a rough idea of when the next one might strike in that area. Some faults break every few years. Some break every one hundred years. Some only break only once every few thousand years.

◀ *The ancient ruins of the town of Beth Shean in Israel, which was destroyed by an earthquake in 749 CE.*

Earthquake prediction is a tricky task. Scientists can identify faults and make theories about when earthquakes will occur, but their predictions are more vague than people would like. It simply is not possible to narrow down a prediction to one day, one week, or even one year. Most faults, even those that break the surface, lie deep underground. Scientists cannot get down to these earthquake zones to see whether the rocks are becoming stressed to the breaking point.

People who live in earthquake zones must deal with uncertainty. In the United States we know that large earthquakes will strike areas in California and Alaska, as well as locations in the Midwest and on the East Coast. We just don't know exactly when.

The colors on this map illustrate the magnitudes of historical earthquakes. Red indicates a magnitude of 7 or higher, orange indicates magnitudes of 5.5 to 7, and yellow indicates 4.5 to 5.5. ▶

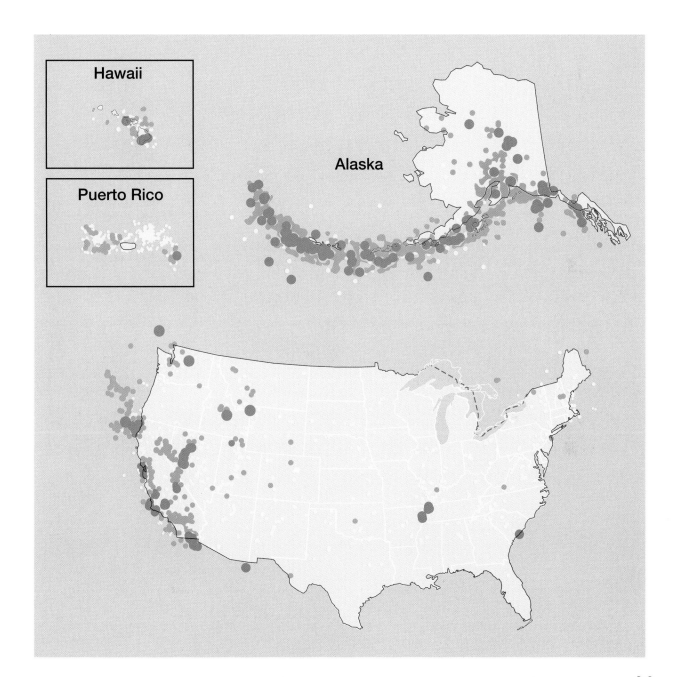

Hawaii

Puerto Rico

Alaska

23

One promising technique for earthquake prediction focuses on "stress triggering." This theory says that every earthquake changes the amount of stress on nearby faults. The changes are small, yet big enough to make some faults break sooner than they might have or to delay future earthquakes in areas where the stress is reduced. Some scientists think that the 1906 San Francisco earthquake took the stress off many faults in the Bay area. The stress-triggering method does not work for day-to-day predictions, but it may alert scientists to those faults that are the most dangerous.

Luckily, the risk of dying in an earthquake is not very high. If you live in a large city, your risk of dying in a car accident is 1 in 4,000. But even if you live in the most earthquake-prone area in the United States, your risk of death from an earthquake is only 1 in 50,000.

These seismic recorders are used to measure earthquakes. Monitoring devices such as these help scientists learn more about earthquakes all over the globe.

Earthquake Damage

Most earthquake damage comes from the power of the seismic waves moving through the ground. The shaking makes buildings sway and sometimes collapse, causes chimneys to fall down, and damages bridges and other structures. Pipelines can rupture, spilling toxic or flammable materials. Fires can start, as happened in the San Francisco earthquake of 1906.

Earthquakes also cause damage along the fault line. If a building stands directly over a fault, it can literally be ripped in half by an earthquake. Roads, fences, and streams that run across fault lines sometimes tear at the fault and separate. A fault running through a dam could cause the dam to fail, flooding the area below.

These buildings collapsed in the 1906 San Francisco earthquake when the ground underneath them slumped. The whole block was later destroyed by fire.

Because of such destruction, earthquakes are among the deadliest of natural disasters. Surprisingly, though, it's not the actual ground shaking that is so dangerous. If you were standing in a field when a big quake hit nearby, you might be thrown to the ground but you probably would not die. Instead, most deaths are caused by collapsing buildings. When a 7.6-magnitude quake hit Pakistan in 2005, at least 86,000 people were killed, largely due to the collapse of buildings in populated areas.

◀ *Rescue workers try to find people trapped in a collapsed building in Pakistan after the October 8, 2005, earthquake.*

Some buildings, such as homes made with wooden frames, can withstand a lot of shaking without falling down. Other types of structures, such as brick or masonry-block homes and apartment buildings, can fall apart unless they are carefully reinforced.

An unreinforced masonry building in Spitak, Armenia, was badly damaged in the 1988 earthquake.

In California the law requires that new buildings be designed to survive earthquakes without collapsing. In other locations, though, such laws do not exist. As a result, great tragedies happen.

For example, compare the effects of the Armenian earthquake of 1988 with the Loma Prieta earthquake in California in 1989. Both quakes had a magnitude of 7.0. The Armenian earthquake killed 25,000 people and destroyed half of the city of Leninakan, while the Loma Prieta earthquake killed only 63 people. Most of the damage in Armenia, located in the former Soviet Union, happened because the buildings were not built well enough to survive a strong earthquake.

◀ Workers reinforce a house in Oakland, California, so it will be more likely to survive future earthquakes.

In December 2003, a devastating earthquake struck the city of Bam, Iran. Scientists in the United States calculated it at a magnitude of 6.7. More than 35,000 people died in the quake, mostly as a result of collapsed buildings. Unfortunately it is very expensive to make buildings safe enough to survive a strong earthquake, so people, particularly those living in Third World countries, will continue to die in large numbers during earthquakes.

Survivors of the 2003 earthquake in Bam, Iran.

Danger from Water: Tsunamis and Floods

On December 26, 2004, the strongest earthquake in more than forty years struck beneath the Indian Ocean. It had a magnitude of at least 9.0 (some have calculated it at 9.3), and set off a devastating *tsunami* that killed at least 295,000 people in countries all across the region.

For people living along the coastline, tsunamis are one of the greatest dangers posed by earthquakes. Tsunamis (sometimes incorrectly called "tidal waves") are powerful waves that can travel long distances. They are created when an undersea earthquake makes the ocean floor shift suddenly. They can also be created by underwater landslides and volcanic eruptions.

◀ *A tsunami wave hits Penang, Malaysia, on December 26, 2004.*

As a tsunami sweeps across the deep ocean, it moves at a speed of more than 400 miles per hour (644 kilometers per hour), making the surface of the water above it rise by just a few feet. When it reaches shallower water, the wave slows down, but the water has nowhere to go but up. It quickly grows higher and sweeps inland before retreating again. Most tsunamis consist of several waves that strike within five minutes to an hour of each other. However, the waves can behave differently in different places.

This satellite photo shows before (top) and after (bottom) views of tsunami damage around Gleebruk Village in Sri Lanka.

For example, during the 2004 Indian Ocean tsunami, the Indonesian city of Banda Aceh was struck by a wave that might have been as high as 80 feet (24 meters), and may have been moving as fast as 30 mph (48 kph). Other places experienced a gentler rising of the water level, but when the water drained back, it swept many people out to sea. Sometimes the first sign of an approaching tsunami is a sudden retreat of water from the shoreline. If you see this happen, move to higher ground as fast as possible.

◀ *Tsunami damage in the town of Meulaboh in the Aceh province of Indonesia.*

Stay Safe

If an earthquake strikes, try to take shelter under a table or other piece of sturdy furniture. Stay away from windows, which can shatter during the shaking. Don't go outside until the quake is completely over; and when you do go outside, stay clear of anything that could fall on you, such as trees, power lines, and damaged buildings. Sometimes a building will survive the main shock but collapse in an aftershock because of hidden damage from the main quake.

If you are near a lake, bay, or ocean, go to higher ground. Remember that a tsunami can consist of several waves, so don't rush back into an area that has just been underwater.

Japanese children practice taking cover underneath a table in an earthquake drill. ▶

Glossary

aftershock—An earthquake that happens soon after a larger quake has struck an area nearby. (A shock before the larger quake is called a foreshock.)

continental plate—A tectonic plate consisting mostly of continental, or land, areas.

crust—The outer layer of the Earth.

fault—A fracture running between two areas of rock in the Earth's crust that allows the rocks to slip past each other.

focus point—The underground location where an earthquake begins, also known as the **hypocenter**.

hypocenter—The underground location where an earthquake begins, also known as the **focus point**. The surface location above the hypocenter is called the epicenter.

magnitude—A measure of the strength of an earthquake.

moment-magnitude scale—A scale for measuring the magnitude of large earthquakes. The moment-magnitude scale is more accurate than the Richter scale.

oceanic plate—A tectonic plate located primarily underneath the ocean; oceanic plates are generally denser and heavier than continental plates, and are thrust downward when the two collide.

Richter scale—A scale for measuring the strength of the seismic waves released by an earthquake.

seismic waves—Waves of energy released by an earthquake. Seismic waves consist of primary (P) waves (which have a forward-and-backward motion and move quickly through the Earth) and secondary (S) waves (which move from side to side and travel more slowly through the Earth). Also known as **shock waves**.

seismograph—A machine used to detect and measure seismic waves.

seismologist—A scientist who studies earthquakes.

shock waves—Another term for **seismic waves**.

subduction zone—A border between an oceanic and a continental plate where the oceanic plate is being thrust beneath the continental plate. The east and west edges of the Pacific Ocean are subduction zones.

tectonic plates—Portions of the Earth's crust that move across the surface of the planet.

tsunami—A powerful wave created by a sudden shift in the ocean floor. It can travel large distances. Tsunamis are sometimes incorrectly referred to as "tidal waves."

Find Out More

Books

Drohan, Michele Ingber. *Earthquakes*. New York: Rosen Publishing Group, 1999.

Gallant, Roy A. *Plates: Restless Earth* (Earthworks series). New York: Benchmark Books, 2003.

Pope, Joyce. *Earthquakes* (A Closer Look series). Brookfield, CT: Copper Beech Books, 1998.

Web Sites

Earthquake Information for Kids

http://www.abag.ca.gov/bayarea/eqmaps/kids.html

http://earthquake.usgs.gov/4kids/

http://www.fema.gov/kids/quake.htm

http://www.seismo.unr.edu/htdocs/abouteq.html

http://www.weatherwizkids.com/earthquake1.htm

About the Author

Joe Thoron is a freelance writer in Washington State. When not writing for children, he builds Web sites and writes marketing copy. He lives on an island north of Seattle, right between several sleeping volcanoes and a major earthquake zone.

Index

Page numbers for illustrations are in **boldface.**